Prayers of
BOUNDLESS
COMPASSION

Prayers of
BOUNDLESS
COMPASSION

JOYCE RUPP

SORIN BOOKS   Notre Dame, IN

www.sorinbooks.com

Paperback: ISBN-13 978-1-932057-16-4

E-book: ISBN-13 978-1-932057-17-1

Cover image © Trinette Reed/Stocksy.com.

Cover and text design by Brian C. Conley.

Printed and bound in the United States of America

Library of Congress Cataloging-in-Publication Data is available.

To

Janet Barnes,

a compassionate
and prayerful woman

with much gratitude
for her constant support

$\mathcal{C}$ONTENTS

$\mathcal{U}$SING THIS BOOK

This book is a companion resource to *Boundless Compassion: Creating a Way of Life* © 2018 by Joyce Rupp. It is available in paperback (ISBN-13 978-1-932057-14-0) and as an e-book (ISBN-13 978-1-932057-15-7). I hope that you are able to benefit from both books.

Many of the prayers and meditations in this book are designed to be used in communal settings. The role of the leader is often specified. Although other roles are not specified, you are encouraged to assign roles such as "reader" and "leader" to members of the group.

Permission to Use Published Material with Acknowledgment

Sorin Books has graciously honored my request that the resources contained in this book may be copied for personal and liturgical use without requiring permission from the publishing company. It is imperative, however, that you give adequate acknowledgment to the source of the piece you are copying. Much published work is lost because of carelessness or hurriedness when the source is not included on a printed page. Copying published work without including the title, author, and publishing company is like visiting the home of a friend and deciding to borrow something valued from that friend's household and then never returning it. Please take the time and have the kindness to acknowledge the source when you print something from this book.

Each page you reproduce must include the following credit line:

COMPASSION AS A WAY OF LIFE

THE BODY OF COMPASSION

I pray to be the face of compassion—
    that those who come within my view
    find a cordial, kindly reception
    written upon my facial landscape.
I pray to be the ears of compassion—
    that those who come filled with distress
    will experience my attentive presence,
    ready to listen without distraction.
I pray to be the eyes of compassion—
    that those who lack society's support
    will receive my nonjudgmental gaze,
    a look of unbiased, heartfelt welcome.
I pray to be the shoulders of compassion—
    that those who come laden with burdens
    will be able to set things down for a while,
    and have the load lightened when they leave.
I pray to be the heart of compassion—
    that those who feel overwhelmed with suffering
    will sense my empathic response,
    one that forgoes a desire to fix the hurt.
I pray to be the mouth of compassion—
    that those whose voice is not heard
    will be empowered and supported
    by my determined, vocal stand for justice.

I pray to be the hands of compassion—
>   that those whose life could benefit
>   from my presence and my actions
>   will be assisted by the humble offering.

I pray to be the feet of compassion—
>   that those who long for companionship
>   will see that I walk beside them,
>   joined in the strength of a common humanity.

I pray that the Light of compassion shining in my soul will recognize and receive the Light shining in others, that together we will care for creation with respect and have gratitude for all that exists.

LET US LOVE ONE ANOTHER

Beloved, let us love one another,
because love is of God; everyone who loves
is born of God and knows God. Whoever does
not love does not know God, for God is love.

—1 John 4:7

Sacred Heart, Love of all Loves,
turn my hesitant heart toward the people
I find difficult to welcome into my life,
especially the obnoxious and arrogant,
the know-it-alls and the have-to-be-rights.
Restore my inner sight to see with your eyes
the people who jolt my visible sensitivity
by their appearance and jarring behavior.
Forgive me for my emotional responses,
and the negative, mental judgments
that betray your expansive compassion.

Take my hand and accompany me
when I encounter snarly, irritable, upset,
and easily angered individuals.
Do not allow me to respond in like manner.
Fortify my kindness with your love
when I am with do-gooders, the self-righteous,
the envious, and the hypocritical.
Regenerate my faith in the goodness of humanity

when I come across betrayers, liars, cheats,
and the least-trusted.

God of Love, let me see myself honestly,
not apart from those I want to shun,
but as another human being among them.
I, too, am in need of transformation.
Love of all Loves, grant that I may grow
in greater awareness of my own
dislikeable traits and disturbing limitations.

May I love others as you love them.
May I find solace in knowing
all of us have a home in your heart,
the Sacred Heart.
May I remember that when I love others
I am loving you.

COMPETITION
AND COMPARISON

*She remembered seeing everything in terms of who
had less than she did and who had more, who was
prettier, smarter, who had a better relationship
(everyone, usually), who was getting promoted faster.
. . . She was constantly trying to figure out how to do
it better, how to get it right, and in doing so she had
started to grind her teeth at night.*

—Ann Patchett, *Commonwealth*

Compassionate One,

When I think poorly of myself because I do not match cultural norms of how to speak, think, look, or act, lead me to acknowledge and appreciate the gifts I have been given. Draw me inward to my core goodness. I will sink into that cradle of kindness and gain strength from what has lasting value.

Disengage my strong connection to the "rush, push, and shove" approach to daily life. Release in me whatever craves to be the best, to rise to the top, to show off who I am and what I can do.

Hush the strong voice of insecurity that steals energy from my spirit. Calm the anxiety that aches to have the spiritual life of another. Lift the darkness from my inner eye so that I see with gratitude how enriched I am in my relationship with you.

Motivate my actions with the purpose of being your voice, your hands, your heart. Instill a steady commitment to share my talents for the benefit of all beings, rather than for how much I will please others, meet their expectations, or merit their affirmation.

Rein in negative, judgmental thoughts that arise from comparing my beliefs and values to those I consider less than worthy. Open any part of my mind and heart that closes the door to respect for those with diverse opinions, theories, and guiding principles.

Teach me how to stand compassionately amid a society that evaluates and labels others as acceptable and unacceptable. Do not let me give in to an adult peer-pressure that would prevent my wholehearted kindness from being extended to others.

In all I am and all I do, keep me mindful that you are the source of my abilities. Humble any form of arrogance or power that leaps into my mindset and brings harm into the life of another person.

Keep circling my heart with your unconditional love until it releases any tendency to compare or compete. Guide my discernment so that I will recognize the subtle ways of wanting more than I need, and be aware when I am seeking superiority over others.

I thank you for all I have been given. I am satisfied with who I am and what I have.

SEEDS OF COMPASSION

To be human is to be compassionate. Scientists now recognize that we are born with the capacity to be empathic and kind. Historians have long been aware of this, having observed the self-sacrificing, generous lives of those who gave their utmost for the benefit of others. Theologians and spiritual leaders have elucidated and encouraged the activation of this virtue, a tenet of every major religion. The seeds of compassion contain great variety, just as a tomato plant comes in an assortment of flavors and shapes. Visit the garden of your heart. Revive the desire to nurture the seeds of compassion within yourself. As you do so, remember you are not alone. The Risen Christ first appeared disguised as a gardener.

Gardener of Hearts, I turn to you today for encouragement and determination in activating the seeds of compassion that have been planted in my being.

Seed of empathy: Awaken my heart to hidden suffering, as well as that which is in full view. Like a seed stirring from the sun's warmth, so may this seed awaken within me.

Seed of solidarity: Keep me attuned to the unity existing within all of creation, to the interdependence we share with one another, existing in similar soils of joy and sorrow.

Seed of nonjudgment: Remind me to pause in my assessment of others, to approach them with a belief in their core goodness, no matter how shrouded this goodness might be.

Seed of forgiveness: Take me to the storeroom of my hurts and disappointment. Assist my efforts to discard whatever urges me to harbor hardness of heart.

Seed of kindness: Refresh my generosity so I can loosen the firm grip on my own time, my own schedule, my own wants, and my own tightly held plans.

Seed of nonviolence: Grant courage as I discover and dig out the weeds of petty irritations, harmful competition, destructive comparisons, and the simmering desire for retaliation.

Seed of just anger: Jostle my peace with a fierce anger, one that demands alleviation of injustices that trample on the human rights of others and destroy their livelihood.

Seed of patience: Pull back the harness on my hurry when I want to see the growth of the seeds of compassion. Help me to entrust their development with the time required.

Seed of sympathy: Turn me toward those who sorrow and grieve. Do not let my fear of vulnerability keep me from bringing comfort that could ease their heartache.

Seed of love: Enable me to love as fully as I can, nurtured by your abiding companionship. Surround and fill my heart with what I need in order to be a compassionate presence.

WALK A MILE IN MY SHOES

The only shoes you can walk in are your own.
With compassion, courage and understanding
we can walk together side by side.

—Michele L. Sullivan, in her TED talk

This meditation can be facilitated by a leader speaking the following words as people sit across from one another, in full view of each other's feet. It is also effective when done alone, whether seated or standing with a group of people (on a bus or train, in a medical waiting room, an office, a family area, waiting in line in a store, or in any public place where you are able to observe unobtrusively the feet of those around you).

THE MEDITATION

Look at your feet. Notice the shoes you are wearing. These shoes are yours. The size fits your feet. Comfort develops once the shoes take on the shape of your feet after you wear them for a while. The longer you use a pair of shoes, the more they surround your feet with "you." The uniqueness of your feet—the short toe or extra-long one, the calluses, corns, bunions, and other imperfections only you know about—form the shape of your shoes. They carry information about you, such as where you walk or run, who you meet, where you go for entertainment, how often you open the refrigerator door, and the steps you take at work. Your shoes know what time of day you slip into them and take them off, when you "put your feet up," or when you kick aside something that gets in the way. They know how long you stand at the kitchen sink and where you shop for food. Your shoes carry the story of "yourself." No one else can fit into those shoes, into your story, in the same way that you do.

Now, look at the shoes of someone else. Gaze at them carefully. Notice the size and shape of his or her shoes. Imagine the "story" they carry, the storehouse of information they contain. If that person's shoes could speak, you would learn so much that is not visible about her or him. You would discover not only exterior aspects but interior ones, as well. Those shoes could have waited in a doctor's office for an unwanted medical report; they may have taken a parent to the graveside of a child; they might have walked out the office door after a coveted position was given to someone else; perhaps they sat silent while the one who wore them sobbed after being betrayed by a beloved partner.

What if you were asked to exchange shoes with the person whose shoes you have just contemplated? Could you wear them comfortably for a day? Would they fit your feet? Most probably not. You would wobble or feel pain if you had them on for very long. So, too, we cannot "wear" each other's stories. We empathize and respect people for who they are and what they have experienced, another human being making his or her way through life as best they can.

Close your eyes now. Think of how easy it is to make snap judgments about another person because of external appearances and behavior. Imagine how much this person whose shoes you gazed upon wants happiness and an ease of life, just as you do. Think of how this person, too, has experienced numerous gains and losses.

If the situation is appropriate, take off your shoes and place them in front of you. Have the other person do the same. Bow to one another with humble respect. Acknowledge the unique story each of you carries. Welcome the bond of humanity that you share.

CONCLUDING PRAYER

Holy One of the Burning Bush, like Moses we take off our shoes.

We are in awe of your presence, not in a fiery bush but in the heart of each human being. Deepen our respect for one another's history of experience, the unique personality and diverse giftedness.

Heal us of quick judgments that are often untrue.

In our relationship with all people may we approach them with respect and a sincere desire to hallow their sacred journey.

Together we stand before you, Holy One aflame in our hearts.

May we walk in peace with each person who comes our way.

2

COMPASSION FOR SELF

THE FEATHER PRAYER

Birds instinctively know how to care for themselves. They regularly groom or preen their feathers so they remain healthy. Birds layer disordered feathers to regulate the wings' balance, pull out tattered and tough feathers to make room for new growth. They pick off parasites, such as lice, that carry disease, and take oil from the base of the feathers and spread it upward for water-proofing. Like birds caring for their feathers, we must also groom our "feathers"—to assure that we stay healthy in body, mind, and spirit.

Find a feather. (If you cannot find one, print an image from the Internet.) Place this in front of you or hold it in your hand. Enter the still-point within yourself. Rest contentedly, remembering the feather is a sign of your desire to care well for yourself.

Winged One of my life, you taught valuable lessons
by observing the birds of the air and flowers of
the field. Be my teacher now as I seek to be self-
compassionate.

I desire to pull out old feathers of negative self-
judgment, to remove tattered remnants of past
thoughts about self that generate discouragement
and lessen positive energy.

Strengthen my daily resolve to layer my activities
carefully, to maintain a reasonable balance of inner
peacefulness.

Sort out with me what old attitudes need to be discarded so that my relationship with you has room enough to grow.

Support me as I pick off the parasites of false expectations, and shake off the collected dust of trying to do too much.

Oil my heart with your love through steadfast prayer and keep me flying freely on the wings of your grace.

May I swim with easy movement upon the sea of your love, float without fretting, and regularly preen my life.

CLOSING

Place one of your hands over your heart. Place the other hand softly, with gentle care, on your forehead. Think of the Holy One extending love to you, desiring the greatest peace and ease for your well-being. Open your mind and heart as fully as you can and let yourself receive this kindness. Now bring your hands back to a resting posture. Sit quietly for a while and allow yourself to rest in this graciousness. Be immersed in the Comforting One's presence.

PSALM 139:
COMPASSION FOR SELF

SAY ALOUD

A group would repeat each of these lines from Psalm 139 after the leader:

- You knit me in my mother's womb.
- I praise you for I am wonderfully made,
- wonderful are your works. (Ps 139:13–14, adapted)

THE MEDITATION

Consider your very early life, the time before you heard anyone say what you could and could not do, before anyone criticized you for what you looked like, how you spoke, what you did. . . . Go back to any early age when you felt free to be yourself . . . a time when you were un-inhibited and lacked fear of criticism . . .

Visualize yourself as this alert, happy child, at ease with life . . .
See yourself free from self-judgment and judgment of others . . .
You are unconcerned about what others think of you . . .
Your whole being is alive with wonder, embracing sounds, colors, shapes, full of trust . . .

All of who you are is eager to enter each moment, unafraid of failing cultural standards . . .

Rest in this freedom of judgment.
Sink into the space where there is no criticism, only loving acceptance and kindness.
Let yourself be held in this cradle of well-being.
Imagine that you are held by the Divine Beloved, as a parent holds a child with tenderness.

SAY ALOUD

- You knit me in my mother's womb.
- I praise you for I am wonderfully made,
- wonderful are your works.

THE MEDITATION

Now picture yourself as you are in your adult life.
Remember the part of you that voices self-criticism and finds fault with yourself.

What are some of the judgmental messages that you give yourself ?

Recall several words you use when making those judgments.

Visualize the Holy One erasing those words.
In place of them you see these words: "You are filled with goodness."

Pause to meditate.

Breathing in: "Goodness in me." Breathing out: "I trust this goodness."

- You knit me in my mother's womb.
- I praise you for I am wonderfully made,
- wonderful are your works.

Close by placing your hands over your heart. Thank the Holy One for accepting and welcoming you with unconditional love.

SELF-ACCEPTANCE
OF ELDERHOOD

Hold a cup, preferably a mug or a coffee cup made of a firm quality, not a thin teacup, as you read or say aloud . . .

May this sturdy cup I hold in my hands
remind me to accept the support of others,
to ask for assistance when I require it,
and to consent to my fading independence.

May the empty space inside the cup
encourage me to accept declining activity,
the slowing down of my body and mind,
my growing inability to be industrious.

May the cup's handle be a sign for me
that I will receive whatever help I need;
with care I can handle unforeseen concerns
and the issues that arise due to my aging.

May the cup's capacity to hold something
remind me of the happy memories I contain;
I can gather their abundance to my heart,
ready at any moment to draw them forth.

May this container I cradle in my hands
assure me of God's love surrounding me;
I am being embraced and supported
by the presence of this Beloved Being.

I hold this cup before me with full confidence,
entrusting my life into the Ancient One's hands.
The One who birthed me safely into this life
will welcome me back home when it is time.

BRIEF MEDITATIONS ON SELF-COMPASSION

MEDITATION 1

Jacob's well was there, and Jesus, tired out by his journey, was sitting by the well.

—John 4:6

Be with Jesus when he comes to the well, weary and in need of rest. Ask him what it is like for him to be there. Then, ask him how you are to sit by your well of life. Listen to how you are to care for yourself.

When you are weary, do you sit by your "well"? If not, what keeps you from doing so? How might you change this? Make an intention to integrate this action into your daily life.

MEDITATION 2

But now thus says [God] who created you . . . you are precious in my sight, and honored, and I love you.

—Isaiah 43:1, 4

Think of the people and situations in your life that lead you to question your inner goodness and beauty. Hold each of these in your open hands and give them over to God. Hear the words of the Holy One in Isaiah 43:1, 4 as if they are spoken to you, here and now. Receive this message as fully as you can, with trust and acceptance. Allow the acceptance and love of the Holy One to flood through your entire being.

MEDITATION 3

A great crowd followed [Jesus] and pressed in on him.

—Mark 5:25

Visualize Jesus standing up for hours to teach the crowds. Imagine how tiring this must have been for him. Imagine the people pushing closer and closer. What is it like to be hemmed in with so little room to move? Notice how Jesus takes care of his need for safety and space as he gets into a boat and sits down a little way out from the shore.

Now, picture a scene from your life when you long to be free from what presses your life too tightly. Invite the Holy One to join you in a boat where you rest and relax. Be filled with ease. Welcome restoration of your body, mind, and spirit from this loving presence as you float gently upon still waters.

MEDITATION 4

Jesus came to Bethany, the home of Lazarus. . . . There they gave a dinner for him. Martha served. . . . Mary

took a pound of costly perfume made of pure nard,
anointed Jesus' feet, and wiped them with her hair.

—John 12:1–3

Imagine you are there in the home of Mary, Martha, and Lazarus. You see how much they love Jesus, how hospitable they are to him. Notice how Jesus receives their kindness and welcomes the loving care they give to him. Reflect on your receptivity when others extend care, kindness, and hospitality to you.

THE FOUR
GUARDIANS MEDITATION

The following meditation offers kinship when we find ourselves in need of an assuring presence, when we long to pray but have a lonely emptiness. At other times, we search for strength to hold us up when we have fallen down and cannot get back up. Even when we turn a corner toward better days and easier communication with the Holy One, the following meditation can be a source of great comfort and peacefulness.

This meditation is based on a belief that it is possible to remain united with the people we respect and admire who have died and now reside in another realm of life. Indigenous communities refer to these persons as "ancestors." Christians call them "saints," those officially recognized for their goodness, and the ones we recognize as the uncanonized saints who also gave witness to living virtuously. In the Church's "Litany of Saints" when we respond "pray for us"; when we call to those whom we refer to as our "guardian angels"; in our personal prayers, calling on good people who left their mark of graciousness on our lives—in all of these ways we have the ability to turn to these deceased, blessed ones, and invite their presence to be with us.

These ancestors, saints, or guardians might be valued relatives, friends, teachers, and others we have personally known, or saints and biblical figures, personages from history, and anyone we might reach out to with an invitation to come and be with us, to bring their loving, wise presence into our sphere of life. They come as comforters, protectors, and guides, providing a circle of safety and calm assurance. They bring strength to go on and encouragement to become more Christlike by accessing our own inner goodness. The guardians' presence carries an unspoken wisdom, and oftentimes a healing we are unaware of needing until it happens.

With this in mind, I invite you to join in this Meditation of the Four Guardians. Do not anticipate ahead of time "who" will show up for you. Simply open your mind and heart, setting aside questions of whether or not this "works," if it is "real," or will be effective.

You are going to invite four guardians, people who have died and gone on before you, to come and gift you with their presence. First, place yourself in a posture of meditation. Begin to enter the quiet space within yourself. Set aside distractions and concerns. As you breathe softly, recede into the deep place within yourself where you trust the presence of stillness and tranquility. Call upon the Holy One for guidance as you enter into this meditation.

THE MEDITATION

Close your eyes. See yourself seated as you now are.

First Guardian

Focus on your right side. Quietly pray, "Come. Come. Come be with me. Come and stand on my right side."

Wait without anxiety for a presence to come to you. You most probably will not picture this person, only have a felt sense or an unspoken awareness of this presence. When you sense that this guardian is there on your right side, imagine a caring arm placed around your right shoulder.

Second Guardian

Focus now on your left side. Quietly pray, "Come. Come. Come be with me. Come, and stand on my left side." Wait with trust for a presence to come to you. Again, you most probably will not "see" or visualize this person, only have a felt sense or an awareness of this presence. When you sense that this guardian is there on your left side, imagine a caring arm placed around your left shoulder.

Third Guardian

Now focus behind your back. Quietly pray, "Come. Come. Come be with me. Come and stand behind my back." Wait for another presence to come to you. When you have an awareness or a sense that this guardian is there behind you, imagine two hands gently placed on top of your head.

Fourth Guardian

Lastly, focus on the space before you. Quietly pray, "Come. Come. Come be with me. Come and kneel before me." Wait patiently, without anxiousness or effort, for a presence to come to be with you. When you sense that this guardian is there, kneeling before you, open your hands and place them palms up before you. Imagine your hands being held by this caring presence.

You are now surrounded, held and embraced, by these four guardians. They care about you. They love you and desire the best for you. Sit quietly and let their loving-kindness and the blessedness of their wisdom seep into every part of yourself, especially your heart. Receive their tenderness and the healing love they bring to you. Accept their strength and wisdom in this circle of safety and love. Receive their qualities. Be as fully present as possible.

Allow for an extended time of quiet.

You will now bid farewell to each of these guardians. Thank them for coming and for what they brought to you. These spirits of goodness will be with you whenever you call upon them. Remember you can invite them at any time in the future. Ask for their blessing and tell them goodbye for now.

Return slowly to this time and place. Be attentive once more to your breath, bringing in the freshness of life and sending forth the restored love in your heart.

Following the meditation, you may wish to do one of the following:

Write a dialogue with one of the four guardians. Ask a question of this person about your spiritual journey.

Write a letter to one of the guardians or have one of the guardians write a letter to you.

3

COMPASSION AND SUFFERING

A PRAYER FOR HEALING

As the various parts of the physical body are mentioned, you may want to place your hand over that area. Visualize God's compassionate light and love moving through that part of your body and outward to those in need of healing.

Healing Presence
fills my body, mind, and spirit;
I receive this healing for myself
with receptivity and gratitude.

Healing Presence
fills my breath;
I send forth this loving balm
to relieve the world's pain.

Healing Presence
fills my eyes;
I send forth a gaze of kindness
upon those who know failure.

Healing Presence
fills my ears;
I send forth a peaceful melody
to soothe cries of lamentation.

Healing Presence
fills my hands;
I send forth a promise
to assist marginalized people.

Healing Presence
fills my mouth;
I speak words of consolation
that release and forgive.

Healing Presence
fills my mind;
I send forth respectful thoughts
and cease harsh judgment.

Healing Presence
fills my heart;
I send forth kindheartedness
to every hurting being.

A MIRROR OF COMPASSION

You may think of compassion as sharing another's
pain. But of what value is that to you or to the other?
If I come to you in pain and you end up with the
same pain, all we have done is add to the world's
suffering. We have done nothing to alleviate it.
I want you to understand my pain, to respond to it
deeply, but not to take it on yourself.
I want you to help me see what you see and what I
cannot see. I want you to engage my pain as if I were
an actor in a drama you were watching. Mirror my
experience, but don't embrace it as your own.

—Rabbi Rami Shapiro

Physician of Souls, Healer of Hearts,
create within me an unwavering resolution
to be a reflection of your unconditional love
as I accompany others in their time of suffering.

Bring teachers of compassion into my life
who will be mentors of dedicated care,
and guides to show me how best to respond.

Be the wisdom I seek in being fully attentive
without being taken over by another's pain.
Keep me aware of wanting to fix or be in charge.

Grant insightful patience so I do not hurry
a healing process, when what it really needs
is sufficient time and sustained gestation.

Journey with me to each one whom I companion;
show me how to mirror your compassion,
to be a reflection of your light-filled presence,
and a reassuring demeanor of understanding.

Move me to enter wholeheartedly into suffering,
while not allowing it to plummet into my soul.
Help me to keep a healthy balance of caring,
as I tend lovingly to others and to myself.

A PSALM OF COMPASSION
(BASED ON PSALM 23)

Caring Shepherd and Guide of My Soul,
many things I want—for self and others:
freedom from worry, healing from hurts,
financial security, health of body and spirit,
sturdy relationships, lasting happiness,
an end of needless suffering and sorrow,
a peaceful planet where everything thrives.

You assure me that I do not have to want;
you will lead me to an inner core of peace
and guide me to ways that restore my spirit.
Suffering will serve as a profound teacher,
a catalyst of empathy and understanding
that unites all who sit at the table of life.

You bid me come to you, to release my fears
and allow you to anoint my worries with trust,
to let you lead me to your resting place
where I can listen to your calm, assuring voice.

No matter how dark the valley of tears,
no matter how unending the turbulence,
you are there with your embracing love.
You are forever a reliant, caring presence.

You breathe your strength into my weakness.
You promise to be a peaceful haven.
You are the home where I can always dwell
in your abiding goodness and compassion.

A REFUGE AND A STRENGTH

> For you have been my help;
> in the shadow of your wings, I sing for joy.
> My soul clings to you,
> Your right hand upholds me. (Ps 63:7–8)

Sheltering One, your voice of care is heard throughout the psalms. Your promise of a comforting refuge resounds in the lives of all who long for peace, and an alleviation of suffering. My heart clings to you for support.

> God makes me lie down in green pastures,
> leads me beside still waters,
> restores my soul. (Ps 23:2)

Refuge for the Lost, bring home the part of my being that yearns to find a resting place in you. Lead me to your still waters.

> How precious is your steadfast love, O God!
> All people may take refuge in the shadow of
> your wings. (Ps 36:7)

Wide Wings of Comfort, wrap your consolation around my sadness when it longs for release. I trust in your faithful love.

> For God will hide me, shelter me in the
> day of trouble. (Ps 27:1, 5)

Cave of Refuge, provide a sanctuary of solace as I wait for the unrecognizable future to reveal itself. Do not let my troubles steal my joy.

> God is my light and my salvation, whom
> shall I fear?
> God is the stronghold of my life; of whom
> should I be afraid? (Ps 27:1)

Home for the Homeless, focus my wayward mind so I concentrate on what is worthy of attention. Keep me aware of the power of my fears to divert me away from you.

> Under God's wings you will find refuge.
> (Ps 91:4)

Welcoming Wings of Concealment, gather me to your heart where I gain strength from the heartbeat of your compassion. Your love sustains me.

> In you my soul takes refuge;
> In the shadow of your wings
> I will take refuge
> Until the destroying storms pass by.
> (Ps 57:1)

Persistent Protector, be the guardian of my mind and heart when destructive, inner storms attack my self-confidence and trust. I lean strongly on your reassurance.

> Lead me to the rock that is higher than I;
> For you are my refuge; a strong tower
> against the enemy. (Ps 61:3)

Source of Strength, stand beside me when I feel weak in body, mind, or spirit. Be my source of stability. I need you to be my strong tower of sure conviction.

CONCLUDING PRAYER

We join our prayer with the psalmist of years past and with the rest of humanity for whom suffering fails to depart. Human need and common experience lead us to gather close to your refuge and strength. Welcome us to the doorstep of your compassion. You are our home, the tender cleft in your divine heart where everyone who suffers finds a welcome. Thank you, Sheltering One, for gathering us under your wings as a mother hen carefully gathers her chicks (Lk 13:34).

REMEMBERING INNER RESILIENCY

Each participant chooses a strong, smooth stone of three inches or more in diameter. They hold the stones as the facilitator leads the meditation.

Take time to quiet your inner and outer self.

Breathe: Notice if your body is at ease, if there is any discomfort, pain, tension, or tiredness. Bring your kindness to this part of your body. Let it know that you care. Breathe peace into this part of your physical self.

Breathe: Be aware of your mind, of anything that is taking peace away from you. Recognize it. Then, ease any disturbance out of your mind. Bring your attention here. Be present to this time and place. Breathe peace into your mind.

Breathe: Be attuned to your spirit. Notice if any emotion you have at this time distresses or preoccupies you. Acknowledge it. Then breathe it out. Let it float away. Be at ease. Breathe peace into your spirit.

Focus on the stone you are holding. This stone is symbolic of your journey with suffering. This stone once had rough, bumpy, sharp edges. Perhaps it was encrusted with clay or other pieces of earth. At some moment in time, it was broken off from a larger layer of stone. During its process of coming to be in your hand, it was tumbled and tossed, bounced around, rolled back and forth, hit by other rocks, and changed by forceful movements on the planet.

Your stone has known all sorts of weather, storms of many types. It has been swept by wild winds, experienced hot sun, and harsh cold. The edges gradually became smooth and easy to touch through the stone's many experiences.

You are like the stone you hold. You have known both calm weather and abrasive storms of life. You have experienced pain and hurt that broke open your heart. Events and situations you did not want to experience have worn your rough edges smoother.

Each time suffering of some form has come your way—whether it be inner struggle with self-acceptance, bleakness in your spiritual life, physical illness, loss of a dream, conflicts in relationships, or sufferings that only you know—each of these has shaped you into the person you now are.

You have gained empathy for others. You share a kinship with everyone who has experienced some kind of hurt. Each painful situation has polished your goodness, buffed your spirit until you shine with ever greater loving-kindness. Your spirit has been refined into a compassionate presence.

Press on the stone. Feel its solidity and strength. It does not bend or break. Like the stone, you have an inner resiliency. You have the power to endure. You can stand firmly in the storms of life.

Wrap your hands tightly around the stone, as if protecting it. Feel how warm the stone becomes as it is sheltered in your hands. In the same way, the warmth of divine love shelters, protects, and comforts you with compassion.

Be still. Experience yourself being encompassed with the Holy One's love.

4

COMPASSION AND MARGINALIZATION

PEOPLE PUSHED TO THE EDGE

Companion of People Pushed to the Edge,
let me stand with the least and the lost.
I will reach out my hand and welcome them.

Let me become one with these sisters and brothers.
I will approach each person as my teacher.

Let me accept their empty, outstretched arms.
I will receive the bounty of their inherent goodness.

Let me come vulnerably close to their distress.
I will try to comprehend the reality of their rejection.

Let me know the breadth of their daily poverty.
I will work for justice that tends to their human
needs.

Let me enter their loneliness and desolation.
I will activate my empathy with compassionate
presence.

Let me acknowledge that my privileged position
is part of the reason they live on the margins.
I will do my part so all may live in one large circle.

Companion of People Pushed to the Edge,
you walk among the ones easily forgotten,
those who are rejected, dismissed, and violated.
Your heart aches for how they are treated
and goes to stand with them on the far borders.

Your love knows no boundaries.
Your love does not judge or tally.

Your love accepts.
Your love gathers.
Your love embraces.

PRAYER FOR REFUGEES

Give me your tired, your poor,
your huddled masses yearning to breathe free,
the wretched refuse of your teeming shore.
Send these, the homeless, tempest-tossed, to me.

—Emma Lazarus

Companion of the Companionless,
let my day not go by without remembering
the sixty-five million people forced from homelands
due to poverty, crime, and political conflict.

Home of the Homeless,
gather the shawl of your compassion
around those who have nowhere to abide,
nowhere to call home, nowhere to work.

Nurturer of the Impoverished,
turn the attention of political leaders
toward systems that cause oppression;
urge them to open their doors to refugees.

Comforter of the Injured,
the prophet Hosea describes your love
as that of a parent lifting a child to her cheek.
Lift, now, the demoralized and beaten-down.

Refuge of the Lost,
protect those who are tossed upon the seas.

Be near to those thirsting in the deserts
and roaming dangerous city streets.

Hope for the Hopeless,
lift up the heavy hearts of families
who have lived for years in camps;
do not let their hope slip away.

Justice Bringer,
bother us. Keep after us. Open our eyes.
Widen our hearts. Change our judgments.
Urge us. Chase us. Badger us, until we act
on behalf of the sixty-five million people
whose tears fall on foreign soil.

TO THE FAR CORNERS

God's compassion is total, absolute, unconditional, without reservation. It is the compassion of the one who keeps going to the most forgotten corners of the world, and who cannot rest as long as there are still human beings with tears in their eyes.

—McNeill, Morrison, and Nouwen,
Compassion

I turn to you, Great Love who goes to those with tears in their eyes, and I pray:

Take my heart to prison cells where there are men and women languishing in unmerited punishment for standing up, speaking out, and courageously seeking justice for those who are oppressed.

Take my heart to impoverished rooms where families have little to eat and parents are growing increasingly despondent from their inability to provide for their children.

Take my heart to women who have been raped, verbally and physically abused, and have nowhere to turn for support and freedom from violent and dangerous situations.

Take my heart to innocent victims of bombings, to those who lie beneath the rubble that used to be their homes, and to the brave, determined first responders who try to rescue the survivors.

Take my heart to each person who, at this very moment, is being trafficked for sex, labor, and any form of domination or enslavement that obliterates self-worth and erases freedom.

Take my heart to each place on the planet where creatures of any size and form suffer because of the ignorance and greed of human beings who treat them as dispensable.

Take my heart to individuals who are addicted to anything that brings harm to their body, mind, or spirit and causes damage to their relationship with others.

Take my heart to people whose depression leads them to be lost in a dark emptiness and to consider suicide as a means to end this desolation.

Take my heart into churches where the doors are blocked to persons whose sexual orientation, personal beliefs, or way of life keeps them from being welcomed.

Take my heart to every parent whose child has a severe disability, to all parents whose child has died, to each parent whose child left home and is lost to them.

Take my heart to medical rooms when men and women are hearing a diagnosis of terminal illness, or a physical condition that will alter forever how they experience their lives.

Womb of Love, take my heart. Shape it with the wide compassion of your heart until I, too, cannot rest as long as there are tears of suffering anywhere on this planet.

WE ARE ONE

*There will not be justice until each person is
satisfied being any person in the world,
in any situation, anywhere.*

—Elizabeth A. Johnson,
Abounding in Kindness

THE MEDITATION

Browse the daily news to find a story of a disenfranchised person, someone who has been forced to the outer edges of society by some type of poverty and exclusion—or select someone from the following list of people on the margins.

a political prisoner sentenced to thirty years' hard
  labor
a middle-aged man addicted to opioids
a blind woman begging on a crowded street
a ten-year-old boy soldier with a rebel group
an undocumented mother of five children
a person with a mental illness who has no financial
  income
a teenager trafficked for sex
a six-year-old orphan in one of the world's largest
  slums
a thirteen-year-old teen in a street gang
a prostitute whose pimp beats her
a homeless alcoholic lying in an alleyway

a widow who has lived for ten years in a refugee
   camp
a father working three jobs to provide for his family
a family living amid the rubble of a bombed village

This reflection offers a way to enter the life of someone on the margins of society when the opportunity to meet in person is not possible. This meditation provides a way to engender empathy and let go of stereotypes that keep compassion locked out.

As you begin to imagine how it might be to live as the particular person you have selected, first set an intention to put aside your personal judgments and biases about him or her. Pause to open your mind and heart to the compassionate Spirit of Jesus. Pray that you will get to know the marginalized person you selected with the kindness that he manifested when marginalized people came to him.

Now, try to picture this person at a certain age. Become him or her as fully as you can. Get to know their physical, external appearance: What do you look like? What ethnicity are you? What kind of clothes are you wearing; do they need washing or mending? Do you also sleep in those clothes? Do you have more than one set of clothing?

Imagine what a typical day is like for you. Where do you wake up? Are you rested? What happens when you wake up? What do you hear? Do you wake up to quiet, to noise, to yelling, to confusion or fear? Do you have a routine or is the morning chaotic? What is the place like where you have been sleeping? Is it cluttered, dirty, or clean? What do you see around you? Do you have furniture? Pictures on the walls? What do you smell? Is the odor pleasant, repugnant, harmful? Are there insects or rodents in your place?

How does your body feel? Is there pain in some part of your physical self? If so, what is the cause of it? Do you have the means to take care of it, to try to lessen the pain or the discomfort?

Do you have water? If so, what is the source of it? Is the water clean? Are you limited in how much water you can use? Are you able to brush your teeth? Can you go to the toilet in private? Is there any place to bathe? Are you physically able to wash yourself or does someone have to help you?

Imagine what you, as this person, are thinking and feeling about your life at this moment. Do you have hope? Are you discouraged? Despairing? Is there anything that brings you joy?

If you go to work, what kind of job do you have? What are the physical conditions like? Are they safe and humane? Does your job pay a just wage? Do you have insurance? How are you treated at work? How many hours do you have to work?

Now, move to the end of the day. Look back and review what the day has been like for you. What time is it when you can finally pause and have time for yourself? How do you feel? Exhausted, lonely, scared, angry, hurt, worried, vulnerable? What are your last thoughts before going to sleep?

If you had one message you could give people who live better lives than you do, what would you say to them?

Close your meditation with the following prayer, or one of your own.

CONCLUDING PRAYER

Holy One, your love unites all of us who live on this planet. We are truly brothers and sisters, joined in spirit through your abiding presence. Gather to your heart all the people who live in situations similar to the person I momentarily became. Enfold all those on the edge of society in your heart of compassion. Guide me to find and enter into actions that will help relieve the burdens of those who are oppressed. Thank you for the immensity of your love.

As an extension of this meditation, at the close you might have the person whose life you entered write a letter to you about his or her situation.

BRIDGING THE WIDE DIVIDE

More than two-thirds of the world's population
struggles for survival . . . while the privileged minority
continues its journey unaffected. . . . Three out of six
people on the planet (3 billion) try to live on $2 a day,
one in six (1 billion) eke out a living on $1 a day.

—Maureen O'Connell, *Compassion*

God of Justice, in this moment of history when civilization remains trapped in the ever-widening divide between "the haves and the have-nots," turn our hearts around and direct them toward compassion. Guide us to do our part in bringing relief and restoration to those in great need. Change the minds and hearts of those who contribute to the wide gulf separating the privileged and the dispossessed. Assist us to do the following as we draw upon the courage and kindheartedness you have planted in the depths of our being:

- Work for changes in governmental structures and regulations so the needs of society's most disadvantaged will be provided.
- Cease blaming "the poor" for their plight and look at the world through their lived experience in order to have empathy, rather than judgment.

- Set aside fear of immigrants and refugees who take up residence in our secure neighborhoods and who open their businesses and shops nearby.
- Recognize when we project an attitude of feeling better than, or more worthy than, people who look differently and act contrary to our social norms.
- Join with community groups working for racial equality and personal safety for every individual, regardless of their ethnicity, religion, and culture.
- Make a sincere effort to establish friendships that encourage getting to know others who do not fit in with the mainstream.
- Give less attention and effort to our monetary gains and more attention to how we can assist others with their daily financial needs.
- Call upon corporations and financial institutions to do their part in alleviating destructive practices that keep people crushed in poverty.
- Share generously of our personal time and talents with organizations dedicated to easing the suffering of underprivileged people.
- Insist that every person have the right to medical attention and education, regardless of position, power, and privilege, or the lack of it.
- Accept responsibility for the aspects of our lifestyles that create the wide divide between rich and poor, and actively do our part to live differently.

Source of All Good, steady our wavering hearts. Buoy up our efforts when we grow discouraged. Keep our focus on your insistence that everyone be given opportunities to provide for their well-being. We want to reflect your kindness. We will do our part.

5
—

COMPASSION FOR CREATION

I BOW TO YOU

The world about us has become an "it"
rather than a "thou."

—Thomas Berry, *The Great Work*

The more humankind approaches creation with a sense of awe,
respect, and appreciation for the beauty and bounty found there,
the less suffering will be generated for creation.

I bow to you, berries on the bush, grapes on the vine, rice in paddy fields, papayas on the tree, corn on the stalk, yams in the ground, and every food source providing life.

I bow to you, healthy bacteria, algae, fungi, protozoa, nematodes, and all organisms nurturing the soil, strong roots and thin shoots, bulbs, fat tubers and generative rhizomes.

I bow to you, feathered ones on your nests, in the sky, on tree branches, and upon the waters, with your cheeps, screeches, quacks, warbles, clucks, and zest-filled songs.

I bow to you, tamed flowers in household gardens, wild ones in meadows, roses in florist shops, blossoms on fruit trees, lotus on ponds, visual feasts of exquisite color.

I bow to you, elements that form planet Earth, the fiery heat at the core, ice at the polar caps, measureless storehouses of minerals, rocks and stones, and veins of precious metals.

I bow to you, reptiles and amphibians, frogs and lizards, salamanders and snakes, alligators and crocodiles, turtles and toads, and every kind of creeping, slithering, swimming creature.

I bow to you, ancient trees standing tall, new saplings taking a first breath, island palms swaying in the breeze, all forms of food-producing trees, silent bushes and shrubs.

I bow to you, burrowing, chewing, and gnawing rodents, porcupines, prairie dogs, lemmings and voles, mice, chipmunks, marmots, gophers, and flying squirrels.

I bow to you, four-legged animals hiding in jungles, feeding on plateaus, grazing across ranchlands, living in forests, wading in streams, and resting beneath banana trees.

I bow to you, insects that pollinate, bugs that bite and sting, fireflies and butterflies, moths and beetles, busy ants and lazy larvae, all winged ones in the soil, water, and air.

I bow to you, black soil, red earth, rocky ground, limestone and granite, ash and cinders, mud and clay, sandy beaches, loamy woodlands, graveled paths and silted streams.

I bow to you, waters of the world, glaciers broad and deep, creeks, waterfalls, ponds, lakes and rivers, immense oceans and small rivulets, narrow channels, mud puddles and harbors.

I bow to you, mountains, rolling hills, volcanoes, valleys, ridges, knobs and plains, deserts, coves, savannas, caves and chasms, cliffs, stony shores, and flat watersheds.

I bow to you, wind circling the planet, bringing oxygen to humans and creatures, feeding plant life with carbon dioxide, clouds gathering moisture to spread upon thirsty land.

I bow to you, fishes of various sizes, colors, and shapes, aquatic mammals such as whales, porpoises, and playful dolphins, seals, manatees, sea and river otters, and the platypus.

I bow with a full heart of gratitude to you, the Holy One, whose generous love cradles all that exists and calls it "good."

LAMENTATION OF ENDANGERED SPECIES

Humans who dwell on planet Earth, we call to you.
Turn your ear to us. Hear our cry for survival.
Open your heart and listen to our pleas.

We fear that we may die long before our intended time.
Do you know us? Are you familiar with our names?
We are the Western Lowland Gorilla, the
     Leatherback Turtle, the Amur Leopard and the
     North Atlantic Whale.
We are the Black Rhino, Mountain Gorilla, and Blue
     Whale.
We are the Sumatran Elephant, the Ivory-billed
     Woodpecker, the Black-footed Ferret, the Tiger,
     and the Green Turtle.
We are the Bluefin Tuna and the Galapagos Penguin.
We are the Polar Bear, Sea Turtle, and Mountain
     Plover.
We are the Macaw, Pronghorn, Swift Fox, and Tree
     Kangaroo, the Dolphins and Porpoises, and
     Monarch Butterfly.
We are the Georgia Aster and the Rafflesia Flower.
We are the Western Prairie Fringed Orchid and
     Arizona Agave.
We are Whooping Crane and Burying Beetle.
The list goes on and on. Many species are already
     gone.

We struggle to continue. We are choked by fishing
   nets.
We search in vain for a safe place to raise our young.
We eat food contaminated with lead from hunter's
   bullets.
Our children die from the plastics that fill their
   stomachs.
The land and waters poison us with their pesticides.
We starve for lack of food no longer present in
   polluted waters.
We are driven from our homes and confused by
   melting ice.
We bear our young and watch them die before they
   grow up.
We wither and fade in soil that no longer provides
   nourishment.
We are overfished, underfed, cast aside, and quickly
   forgotten.

Hear us, people of our planet. We are your sisters. We
are your brothers. Hear our cry to live. Hear our ap-
peals to share the benefits of this planet. We, too, cher-
ish life. We, too, deserve to live. We, too, are worthy of
care and consideration. Respect us. Give us a chance.
Change your way of living so we can live. Hear our
cry for life.

Hear us!

MEDITATION ON A PEBBLE

For this meditation each participant will need a small pebble to hold.

Look at the seemingly insignificant pebble you are holding in your palm. You could easily pass by this little thing, or not notice stepping on it. Look closely at the color, the pebble's shape, size, and texture.

Imagine the amazing journey this small bit of creation has taken. You are holding in your hand a piece of stardust from billions of years ago. The elements of this small pebble have come from somewhere in the universe. A star composed of gases exploded and was strewn into space; it eventually formed hot lava that became the planet we call Earth. Ever so slowly this mixture became solid, creating an outer crust on the planet. This crust developed into solid layers of rocks composed of minerals.

What you hold in your hand is some of the earliest part of our planet. Look closely at your pebble: Where was this pebble's first home? How many homes did it have? Was it part of an upheaval of minerals that shaped into a mountain? Did it experience being within a volcanic eruption? Was it at the bottom of a lake? In the seam of a glacier? Did a river carry it along for thousands of miles? Has it been washed out from a dark cave? Pause for a while to think about the long history of this seemingly insignificant thing.

This pebble has known a journey of dissolving, joining, shaping, becoming part of a solid, large form and then a smaller and smaller one. It has known a lot of history in its expansive life. If your pebble could speak, it would have a lot to say to you. Listen for a moment to what it might speak to you if it could.

What you hold in your hand may seem dead but it has its own life, a small electromagnetic field of energy. You cannot detect this but scientists know it is there. Pause to look again at what you hold, an invisible, unfelt energy that carries an ancient history filled with stories.

Lift the pebble to your cheek. Let its sacredness touch you. Welcome your union with the long-evolving history it has known. This little pebble is allowing you to touch a star.

Bring the pebble away from your face and down to your lap. Continue to hold it in your palm. Give thanks to the Creator for its existence and message, for how it tells you of the sacredness of even tiny, seemingly inert things.

Take the pebble with you and place it in your home or office where you can behold it when your sense of wonder and gratitude weakens. Let it remind you of the sacredness of everything that exists.

WE DO NOT OWN
THE LAND AND SEAS

We ponder your steadfast love, O God,
in the midst of your temple.
Your name, O God, like your praise,
reaches to the ends of the earth.

—Psalm 48:9–10

Creator of Beauty and Abundance,
our planet Earth is your sacred temple,
a circling blue and green orb of splendor,
a splash of color in the Milky Way Galaxy.

This wonder of the spacious heavens
has been carved into sections and segments,
divided by humans' insistent domination.
They have failed to understand and accept
that the land and the waters belong to you,
a gift to all humans and all nonhumans—
never to be fought over, bartered, and bought.

MY lawn, MY beach, MY country, MY lake,
MY minerals, MY forests, MY mountains.
When did the illusion of "my" overtake
the eternal truth that all of Earth is yours?

Giver of All Good, Benevolent Being,
teach us to return what is falsely owned,
to let go of our territorial persistence;

awaken us to share what you have gifted:
a temporary home, a lovely place on loan.

Guide and direct us to change our views.
May we have the courage to finally set free
what we humans have wrongfully claimed
as belonging only to ourselves.

WHAT HAVE WE DONE TO THEM?

Shoot them. Swat them.
Stomp on them. Kill them.
Steal their food. Beat them.
Rip the hide from their bodies.
Get them out of the way.
Cage them. Slaughter them.
Poison them. Drown them.
Hook them. Snare them.
Cut off their paws. Skin their fur.
Squash them. Behead them.
Bleed them. Kill them.
Weed them out. Cut them down.
Work them to death.
Trap them. Mutilate them.
Saw off their tusks.
Catch them. Starve them.
Stuff their dead bodies
and display them on a wall.

Snakes, spiders, bats, rodents.
Doves, deer, elk, and moose.
Exotic animals killed for sport.
Innocent ones straying into towns.
Raccoons looking for food.
Beetles, worms, and bunnies.
Geese, ducks, any feathered fowl.
Wolves, coyotes, and cougars.

St. Francis of Assisi called each one
a "brother" and a "sister."

What have we done to our family?

6

Compassionate Presence

ACTIVATING THE FRUITS OF THE SPIRIT

The fruit of the Spirit is love, joy, peace,
patience, kindness, generosity, faithfulness,
gentleness, and self-control. . . .
If we live by the Spirit, let us
also be guided by the Spirit.

—Galatians 5:22, 25

Come, Spirit, assure us that the turbulent animosity
and violence of this era can be lessened when we
express your *love* in our attitudes and actions.

Come, Spirit, plant an emergent *joy* in the hearts of
those who seek relief from the daily drudgery of
poverty, discrimination, and societal indifference.

Come, Spirit, weave your *peace* through leaders
of nations whose governance supports and
encourages domination over other human
beings.

Come, Spirit, slow us down when we lack *patience*
to be with people whose pain would lessen if we
brought our compassionate presence.

Come, Spirit, soothe our soreness of mind and heart
with touches of *kindness* that heal and restore our
desire to be considerate of others.

Come, Spirit, open our hands and hearts to go
beyond a fear of scarcity, to share *generously* from
what we have to assist people in need.

Come, Spirit, draw back home to *faithfulness* anyone
who is straying from vowed commitment and
lost in the illusion of self-centeredness.

Come, Spirit, awaken those who consider *gentleness*
of heart a weakness; help them see how this
virtue reflects your enduring strength.

Come, Spirit, tame our sanctimonious voices with
self-control when we are caught in judgmental
opinions and haughty condemnation.

Rushing Breath of Love, you came into the Upper Room
of the disciples long ago, calming their fears, encouraging
their vision, and enlivening their ability to be people of
valor, compassion, and healing. You come into the Inner
Room of our lives today, offering us this same transforming gift. Open what is closed within us. Breathe renewed
confidence into our fatigued spirits. Send us forth with
a passionate intention to be conveyors of your unconditional love.

TREASURE IN EARTHEN VESSELS

*We hold this treasure in earthen
vessels, that the surpassing power
may be of God and not from us.*

—2 Corinthians 4:7

Much in this world bears suffering that appears to be insurmountable or unavoidable. As some of this pain is spoken in the following statements, we turn to the hope-filled strength expressed in 2 Corinthians 4:7. Let us not forget that we are these vessels, carrying within us a magnificent presence. This grace-laden energy imbues our being and carries our hope when it wavers.

Respond after each of the following with "We are your earthen vessels. We contain your surpassing power."

- Difficulties come and go. Stand confidently amid what does not seem to change.
- Sorrows seep into the fabric of souls with the weight of a formidable anchor.
- Depression clangs the prison door shut on laughter and thrives in the darkness.
- Financial problems menace minds and prey like hungry vultures on inner peace.
- Climate change wreaks havoc on the weather and brings more destruction.

- Strangers once welcomed with joyful hospitality are shoved away with fear.
- Family relationships shift from love to harsh anger like sand on the seashore.
- No amount of compassion seems to ease the suffering caused by violence.
- Children leave behind the values and religious inheritance they received.
- Marriages "made in heaven" now transition to ones of destructive hatred.
- Old memories rise up like silent volcanoes to spew the lava of past abuse.
- Changes accompanying elderhood steal long-treasured energy and memory.
- Parents discover the child they love has turned from them toward drugs.
- People of privilege resist the reality of the great divide between rich and poor.
- Suicide bombers remain convinced that what they choose is God's will.
- Mean words, quick tempers, and thoughtless rhetoric tear apart reputations.
- Prayer that once nurtured and uplifted now hides in persistent hibernation.
- Political divisions rip apart a society once joined in a shared purpose of unity.

- Everywhere it appears that common kindness and human decency are lost.

Together:

Spirit of Compassion, you restored the dying hopes of those who felt discouraged in the Upper Room after the death of their beloved Teacher. Surprise us with an awareness of your transforming presence. Restore our hope day by day as we remember the power of love we carry within us. We have the ability to change the tide of the times. Your compassion moving through us can do more than we can ask or imagine (Eph 3:14–21).

GROWING SEEDS OF COMPASSION

This is a reflection on the seed of compassion within us. You will need a seed for this meditation.

THE MEDITATION

Hold the seed in your hand. Be aware of the potential for growth within it. Sense the energy for new life that it contains. This life cannot be seen. Yet, we trust in its presence. We "take it on faith," and believe in the possibility.

The seed goes into the earthen darkness. There it receives moisture, warmth of sun.

These elements soften and open the hard shell.

You have the seed of compassion stored in you. The potential to develop compassion exists there, to grow in caring, understanding, nonjudgment, forgiveness, kindness, peacefulness, nonviolence.

Look into your current life situation. See someone who could benefit from your compassion. This person might be someone at home, at work, a political figure, or a group of people.

How can the seed of your compassion grow there?

Receive the grace, the energy of the Holy One, to stretch into life, to be a compassionate presence.

Breath Prayer

On the in-breath, silently say: "Seed of Compassion."
On the out-breath, silently say: "Growing in me."

Concluding Prayer

A Creed for Sowing Seeds of Compassion

I believe that the sun drawing green into tiny leaves is much like the Spirit of Love drawing forth compassion from within me.

I believe the call to be a loving presence is a privilege and a gift; that the seed of compassionate presence dwelling in the soil of my heart waits to be nurtured and brought into life.

I believe that compassion has often been planted in my life because of another who nurtured and grew the seed of kindness, and shared that harvest with me.

I believe that great things come from even the tiniest seed of compassion if I plant the seed with generous love and carefully tend it.

I believe that trust and hope are essential in growing the seed of compassion because I may not know what sprouts and grows in the hidden soil of my loving-kindness.

I believe it takes much patience to grow a seed of compassion, to allow it to take root and develop in its own good time and in its own way.

I believe in the Sower of Compassion, in the Great Love who nurtures and sustains the growing process in every caring heart of compassion.

INDWELLING LIGHT

*You are the light of the world. A city built on a hill
cannot be hid. No one after lighting a lamp puts it
under the bushel basket, but on the lampstand, and it
gives light to all in the house.*

—Matthew 5:14–15

Light a candle. Turn off the artificial lights so the room contains as much darkness as possible. Hold the candle between your hands. Notice how the light of this candle reaches and stretches out, dispelling the darkness.

Place one of your hands over the candle you are holding. Feel the amazing warmth this one candle produces.

This small light in your hands is a reminder of the much greater Light that fills your entire being. You have within you the gift of a transforming love, a compassionate warmth that can spread forth like the light of the candle. Pause to be with this presence of Light and Love dwelling within you.

This Light not only fills you, it extends beyond you, reaching out to influence those who pass by you, those who enter your physical space. *(If you are with others, hold the candle out for them to feel the warmth it emits.)*

Pause to be attentive to the pattern of your breathing, to the quiet, steady rhythm, the movement in and out.

Just as your breath goes out from you, the healing energy of Abiding Light and Transforming Love moves forth from you. Visualize someone you know who is hurting. See them slowly passing by you. As you visualize this movement, send forth Healing Light to this person.

You may wish to bring other people to mind who could also benefit from this healing. Visualize each one passing by you, being a receptor of the Compassionate Light streaming forth from within you.

Notice your hands holding the candlelight. Stand up and extend the candle outward in front of you. Hold the light there as you make an intention to be a healing presence for those who come into your life.

Thank the Holy One for the bountiful gift of abiding Light within you.

CONCLUDING PRAYER

Indwelling Light, I desire to share your healing presence abiding within the temple of my being. Just as physical light spreads out to reach as far as it can, so may your Light within me be a transforming energy of healing for those who suffer.

SENDING FORTH COMPASSION

I stand at the door of a light-filled dawn
where the gift of hope rises in my soul.
I open my heart and send forth this gift
to each and every person longing for joy,
to all whose spirit grows dim with sorrow.

I stand at the window of midday
where the flurry of the day's activity
beats upon the pane with urgency.
Opening my heart to where peace resides,
I send forth this abiding harmony
to all who are caught in the claws of poverty,
whose endless work seems never enough.

I stand at the gate of the lengthening dusk,
the transitional place between light and dark;
I send forth confidence from my heart
to those who are unsure in their transitions,
to each person who questions the future.

As I stand at the entrance of the dark night
I open my heart to send forth compassion
to those whose body or mind knows pain,
to all whom the nighttime brings burden, not rest.

Throughout the day and into the nighttime
I stand with the Holy One by my side, calling out:
"Peace to one. Peace to all. Hope resounding.
Love indwelling. Compassion abounding."

7

OTHER PRAYERS OF COMPASSION

THE SOUND OF THE BELL

May the sound of this bell
penetrate deeply into the cosmos.
In even the darkest spots,
may living beings hear it clearly,
so their suffering will cease,
understanding arise in their hearts,
and they can transcend
the path of anxiety and sorrow.

—Thich Nhat Hanh

Bells. They call to worship and prayer, precede meditation, awaken sleepers, invite to dinner, ring out in monasteries, signal the hour on clocks, and indicate all sorts of hellos and goodbyes, beginnings and endings. Each gong or ringing of the bell emits a sound composed of invisible vibrations. These move through the air and into our receptive ears.

Love is an energy. Like the sound of a bell, it carries unseen vibrations. This energy is received, felt in the heart, sensed in the mind. When we send forth love from our hearts, we send forth a resonance that can reach far and wide, like a bell ringing in our heart.

The stronger the love, the stronger the resonance. The mightier the intention, the further the extension of this vibrating energy.

Ring a bell. Listen to the resonance of the bell's
   sound.
Place your hand over your heart. Feel the steady
   rhythm of the heartbeat.
Your love, like the heartbeat, engages with the
   rhythm of indwelling, divine love.
Intentionally send forth this love to someone you
   know who is suffering.

Ring the bell again. Listen to the vibration of sound
   going forth from it.
Place your hand over your heart. Feel the steady
   heartbeat.
Let the love within you grow fuller, your intention
   stronger.
Intentionally send the resonance of this love into the
   larger world.

Ring the bell one last time. Let the resonance be a
   prayer of hope.
Let this hope ring out, resonating in the hearts of all
   who long to hear it.
Place your trust in this transforming power of divini-
   ty to touch a heart,
to change a life, to reach the furthest regions where
   suffering exists.

SEED PACKETS OF COMPASSION

For this meditation experience you will need to select a small, transparent container such as a pill pouch or a simple plastic bag. Select four seeds of your choice, any size, any type. These seeds are to represent various aspects of compassion that you will be practicing for the next six weeks. (That is the amount of time people spend with the companion volume to this one, Boundless Compassion, *a course of study and discovery designed to last six weeks.)*

Place the seed packet in a place where you will see it each day, hopefully several times a day. This might be on your kitchen table, an office desk, taped to a bathroom mirror, in a book you read each day, or on the dashboard of your vehicle. Every week place the packet in a new position or place in order to stay alert to it.

Week 1: Hold the seed packet as you sit quietly. The potential for growth in the seeds is like the potential within you for growing in compassion. Look at the seeds. Each one represents one of the four basic components of compassion: Nonjudgment, nonviolence, forgiveness, and mindfulness. Focus on these four qualities this week. Hold the seed packet each day and pray the following prayer, or one of your own:

Compassionate Gardener of My Heart, I desire to grow in being compassionate. Keep me aware of opportunities to practice this virtue today. May your love draw forth goodness in me the way sunshine draws forth life from a seed. I entrust my desire to be a person of compassion into your care.

Week 2: Hold the seed packet as you sit quietly. This week the seed packet reminds you to be compassionate toward yourself. Reflect on ways that you neglect this kindness to your body, mind, or spirit. Choose one way in which you will practice being more self-compassionate in the coming days. Close by praying to the Compassionate Gardener of your heart.

Week 3: Hold the seed packet as you sit quietly. This week the seeds remind you of the love you have within you that can comfort people who suffer. Choose one person or group of people to unite with in your prayer. As you hold the packet, send forth loving-kindness from your heart to an individual or group of people who are suffering. Bring care and comfort this week to someone who suffers. Close by praying to the Compassionate Gardener.

Week 4: Hold the seed packet as you sit quietly. This week the packet of seeds represents the ways in which you can be united with people who are on the margins of life. Choose a person or group who experience impoverishment, prejudice, or some other hardship that keeps them at a distance from society's acceptance. Send forth love from your heart to that individual or group. Look for opportunities each day to reach toward persons on the margins. Close by praying to the Compassionate Gardener.

Week 5: Hold the seed packet as you sit quietly. The seeds this week represent your ability to grow in an appreciation of nature and to be more aware of the suffering found there. Let the seed packet remind you to do one thing each day that will benefit our planet (recycle, be careful of water usage, be grateful for what you eat, walk instead of drive, etc.). Close by praying to the Compassionate Gardener.

Week 6: Hold the seed packet as you sit quietly. This week return to the four basic components of living compassionately that you focused on in Week 1. Each day choose one way to live compassionately by being nonjudgmental in your thoughts, by forgiving someone for a grievance, by not harboring a desire for revenge or retaliation of any type, and by being more conscious of how you can lessen or alleviate the suffering of others in some way. Close by praying to the Compassionate Gardener.

At the close of these six weeks, take the seeds in the packet and plant them in a pot or outdoors where you can watch them come to life, while your compassion continues to grow and mature.

RELEASE WHAT BLOCKS COMPASSION

Response: May we be compassionate as the Holy One is compassionate.

We have clearness of mind and heart, recognizing what gets in the way of our intention to be a reflection of divine love . . .

> *All*: May we be compassionate as the Holy One is compassionate.

We let go of that which steals our peace, contributes to our apprehension, and keeps us from conveying harmony when we are with others . . .

We recognize unfair judgment when it arises and set it aside quickly, so that we may welcome others with openness . . .

We release any negativity that keeps us from offering kindness to the part of ourselves that longs for empathy and understanding . . .

We relinquish some of our valued time and energy in order to enter the lives of others whose suffering awaits our compassionate presence . . .

We step away from impatience, blaming, unwarranted irritation, and other emotional responses that block our ability to be a caring person . . .

We find within us the courage to let go of fear when it holds us back from speaking or standing up for people who suffer injustice . . .

We let go of anything that prevents us from being faithful to our spiritual practice, so that our compassion remains fresh and ready to be shared . . .

All: We turn to you, Compassionate One, trusting that you will restore our loving-kindness when it is depleted. Guide us in knowing what is required and what needs to be released. Place within us a strong hope that you are there with us whenever we choose to be with those who suffer. You are our strength and companion of love. Thank you for moving our spirits toward ever deeper, fuller, and more enduring compassion.

THE GIFT OF COMPASSIONATE CAREGIVING

Heartfelt Expression of Compassion, you continually care for each of us. Thank you for the gifts that kindheartedness elicits. Help us recognize the unforeseen benefits arising from generous service and empathic presence. May our desire to manifest your compassion keep enlarging the capacity of our hearts. Thank you, especially, for these gifts of caregiving:

- Developing dormant skills and abilities that would otherwise be left unexpressed.
- Observing the faith-filled strength of persons suffering from undiminished pain.
- Recognizing how much we receive from the recipients of our constant care.
- Cherishing the individual traits and endearing qualities of those we serve.
- Standing in the Hallowed Chamber of Love when divine light radiates in another.
- Rejoicing when someone's deep-rooted, psychological wound begins to heal.
- Leaning heavily on the strength of Divine Grace when all seems lost or useless.
- Remaining faithfully present to those with ongoing loss and suffering.

- Witnessing forgiveness, and the calm serenity and peacefulness that follow it.
- Experiencing being held by you, Holy One, while walking with the heartbroken. Observing peaceful surrender in the dying as they enter their final days.
- Discovering new friendships and savoring valued ones from past caregiving.
- Gaining greater wisdom from elders as they bravely face diminishment.
- Learning from the resolve of the sorrowful to heal from their extensive grief.
- Gleaning clearer insight about personal identity and professional purpose.
- Seeing small glimmers of joy break through dense clouds of despair.

Pause now, and reflect on other gifts that have come to you in the process of caregiving. Mentally gather the abundance of what you have received. Hold these gifts close to your heart with gratitude.

Thank you, Provider of Plenty, for each and every gift that flows from the daily tasks and duties of being a caregiver for others. Remind us often when we feel depleted to look at what we have received. Nurture and strengthen our resolve to be a compassionate presence, the kind of presence that manifests your love to everyone in our care.

GROWING IN COMPASSION

*A peaceful mind, not one in contention with anything,
is a possibility for human beings. This doesn't mean
a mind that likes everything or even is indifferent to
everything. It means a mind that has
come to understand that contention produces
(indeed is) suffering. It means a mind able,
through clarity, to choose a wise response.*

—Sylvia Boorstein

THANK YOU, HOLY ONE

Thank you for my brain and its amazing possibilities for growing in peace and well-being.

Thank you for an ability to be aware of my thoughts and feelings, my desires and aversions.

Thank you for the times I have made choices for my own good and the good of others.

Thank you for being able to recognize what motivates my responses to difficult situations.

*The path to happiness and well-being never ends.
Just when we think we've arrived a new challenge
presents itself and we begin again.*

—Christopher Germer

FORGIVE ME, HOLY ONE

Forgive me for being preoccupied with my own wants, and failing to recognize the concerns of others whom I could have assisted.

Forgive me for hanging onto disparaging thoughts about people whose appearance and mannerisms did not meet my standards for how to live.

Forgive me when I refused to release my tight hold on material things, and did not share my abundance with people who have much less than I do.

Forgive me for turning away from opportunities to add my voice to those crying out for justice and a fair life for everyone on this planet.

Peace I leave with you; my peace I give you.
Not as the world gives, do I give to you.
Do not let your hearts be troubled or afraid.

—John 14:27

HELP ME, HOLY ONE

Help me to develop positive habits that lead me to be an oasis of compassion.

Help me to go beyond instinctual fear, flight, and fight, and move toward peace.

Help me to remember that you will lead me to what is best for myself and others.

Help me to trust that I can find happiness, even if life does not always go as I wish.

Our soul rests in God its true peace;
our soul stands in God its true strength,
and is deep-rooted in God for endless love.

—Julian of Norwich

GUIDE ME, HOLY ONE

Guide me when I need to turn from busyness and be more in touch with my inner life.

Guide me when I want to hold onto my self-oriented ways instead of your Way.

Guide me when I look for greater peace and harmony within and beyond myself.

Guide me when I lose my intention of being a person of boundless compassion.

THE JOURNEY OF COMPASSION

REFLECTION 1

Jesus walks with the two who are feeling defeated.
Read the Emmaus story in Luke 24:13–35.

Imagine how it must have been for Jesus to hear their sadness and disappointment.

What was it like for the two when they expressed their thoughts and feelings to him?

If you were to describe this as "a walk of compassion," what aspects would you include?

Where do you find compassion for yourself and others in this story?

When someone walked with you when you were hurting, what part of that "walk" did you most appreciate?

REFLECTION 2

Go for a slow walk. Call to mind a compassionate person whom you admire. This could be anyone from the canonized saints, a person from the Bible, literature, or history, or someone you know personally. Imagine you are walking in this person's shoes when he or she meets someone filled with hostility. How would the compassionate figure you have chosen respond to the situation? Notice the details of thought, feelings, action. What might you learn and benefit from this compassionate person?

REFLECTION 3

Look at your feet. Think about the journey of life they have been on since the time you learned to walk. What are five central beliefs from your family, religion, and culture that form a base out of which you think and act? How has this history of yours fashioned and influenced your experience of compassion?

If you could walk backwards into your life, is there anything you might change in regard to offering compassion to yourself and others?

If you were drawing on your shoes in an attempt to depict some aspect of yourself as a compassionate person, what is the central slogan (words or art) that you would put on each shoe?

CONCLUDING PRAYER

Companion on the Road of Life, no matter how long or short the distance of the journey, you stay by my side. Thank you for your encouragement when the road is challenging and the view ahead is hazy. I can walk with hope in my heart, knowing you are with me whether the way is hilly or straight, rough or smooth, blocked or open to easy access. I walk with your compassion, a love that comforts and strengthens me with every step I take.

EXTERNAL AND INTERNAL STILLNESS

PHYSICAL SELF

With a gentle, inward attentiveness, review your physical self and see if there is any part that has pain or discomfort, any place in your body that does not hold peace. Pay special attention to the back, hips, head, legs, stomach. Direct your kindness to your physical self and embrace this part of you with compassion.

MENTAL SELF

Be attentive to your mind. Notice what seems to be predominant in your thoughts—any concerns, unresolved issues, pessimism—anything in your mind that keeps peace from flowing through you. Visualize a place where you can go to be at peace, perhaps in nature, sitting in a chapel, your place of prayer, in your garden, anywhere that you can be mentally contented. Direct your kindness to your mind and embrace this part of you with compassion.

EMOTIONAL SELF

Take inventory of how you are feeling. Observe emotions that keep your inner self from stillness, any anxiety, lack of harmony—anything that keeps you from feeling at home with yourself. Sense a warm, flowing energy of loving-kindness move through your whole being. Start with the top of your head and move this peaceful, comforting love through yourself. Allow this gentle release of peace to find a home in each part of your being. Direct this kindness to your emotional self. Embrace this part of you with compassion.

SPIRITUAL SELF

Focus on the center of your being, the essence and core of who you are, your deep self. Here Divine Light resides. Open and allow yourself to be enveloped by this Great Love. You are welcomed with total acceptance. Receive the kindness of this beloved Being and sense your deepest self being embraced with compassion.

CLOSING MEDITATION

Enter into stillness. Receive the flow of Divine Love coming in with your in-breath and going out to the world on your out-breath. Remain in this prayerful posture of giving and receiving Love for as long as you wish. Bring this meditation to a conclusion by placing your hands over your heart in a gesture of gratitude, with an intention to be a compassionate presence throughout the day.

RECOVERING LOST QUALITIES OF COMPASSION

Gather and fill a basket of dried leaves. Each person takes a leaf.

Look at the leaf in your hand. Study the lines, the shape, the texture, the edges, the color.

Now close your eyes. Imagine the leaf as it looked when it was full of life on a tree, a plant, a bush.

Visualize the leaf gradually losing color and becoming less vibrant.

Sense how it begins to lessen in vigor and energy.

See a strong wind shake it, tossing it back and forth . . . and now the leaf you hold in your hand falls to the ground, slowly fading in color, ready to decompose in the soil.

Open your eyes and look again at the leaf in your hand. Let it be a symbol of something in your life that was once energized and animated your compassion, but has now become that which needs to fall away, like the leaf falling and fading into the soil. It has to be let go, so it can be transformed into energizing compassion again.

Perhaps your patience has become impatient.
Maybe your peacefulness has gotten lost in anxiousness.
Perhaps your forbearance has become judgmental and critical.

Your generosity might be squeezed into a tight withholding.

Your joy may have turned into deadening boredom and defeatism.

Perhaps your loving-kindness has faded and become self-centered.

Pause to consider if any part of your practice of compassion has become a dried leaf that needs to be transformed.

If and when you find that aspect, take the leaf and place it in the basket with the intention of restoring the quality of compassion that has faded or been lost.

CONCLUDING PRAYER

Good Shepherd, you sought out the lost. When you found them, you rejoiced. When I lose essential dimensions of compassion, guide me to seek them out. Rejoice with me when I find them. Enliven my hope of restoration. Help me to keep the qualities of compassion close to my heart and active in my life.

TWIG MEDITATION

This meditation led by a facilitator requires a basket of small twigs that have fallen from a tree. Each person chooses a twig from the basket.

Become familiar with this twig. It will be your teacher today. Look at the color and size, the markings and the bark, the ends of the twig where it has been broken off from the branch that gave it a home.

The twig you hold began its life as a small protrusion from a branch. It received nurturance from the roots of the mother tree as the food was carried through the tree to this twig.

The sun warmed the twig. The rain washed it. The clouds protected it from too much heat. Birds and other creatures sat on it. Insects used it as their pathway and their home.

This twig went through the seasons of the year while it was attached to the tree, but something happened in its life to separate it from where it belonged. Perhaps a strong wind or an ice storm—maybe it did not receive enough nurturance and became too weak to remain as it was.

What must it have been like to be ripped away or pushed from its source of life, to have left where it had union, nurturance, and the benefit of belonging to a larger community of branches?

While this twig can never rejoin the tree again, it now enters another journey, one that will eventually be life-giving. The twig will slowly decay, becoming humus, rich soil for seeds to grow and be nurtured.

Although what you hold appears dead and inert, it actually holds the potential for life.

Someday this twig will become the birthplace for green grass, flowers, perhaps vegetables.

Let this twig be a metaphor for your life, for some part of yourself that you have known and valued, that connected you to a greater dimension of life and is now broken off. This might be a part of your body, a person, a belief, a profession, a marriage, any valued aspect of your life that has been broken away from your life.

Enter into this disconnection or lost aspect, the separation from what you held onto, or what held you. Reflect on the letting go that this disconnection required of you.

Open your mind and heart to how this loss, like the twig, will someday be a source of something new for you, perhaps greater compassion, deeper communion with the Holy One, more understanding of others who suffer loss. You may already have come to see what this newness is. If not, trust that in time something will be birthed.

Close your eyes. Unite with the Holy One. Listen for anything else you are to learn from the twig. Then offer your prayer of thanksgiving for the teachings that came from reflecting on the twig.

STEPPING FORWARD

Whoever claims to abide in Jesus
ought to walk just as he walked.

—1 John 2:3–11

Stand for this prayer. With each of the following statements, take one step forward.

- I step forward in my life with a desire to be a compassionate presence.
- I step beyond what stops me from bringing loving-kindness to those whose lives are in need of it.
- I step into our hurting world with a realization of my profound connection with each suffering part of it.
- I step with a renewed intention to be open-minded in my thoughts and attitudes toward those who differ from my views and way of life.
- I step ahead with openness to receive compassion from those offering support when I go through life's difficulties.
- I step readily into daily tasks and responsibilities, trusting that whatever is done with kindliness and consideration can be of significant value.
- I step past my hesitations and inadequacies, trusting I have within me what I need to be a compassionate presence.

- I step with determination to do my part to bring about justice to the most vulnerable and forgotten members of our planet.
- I step confidently toward the unknown events and experiences awaiting me, believing that I contain the Holy One's lantern of compassion in my heart.

Add your own "steps" to this list . . .

CLOSING PRAYER

Divine Gate-Keeper, ever present to my soul,
As I approach the open gate of life each day,
Keep me aware of how I can be compassionate.
Your wisdom directs each of my inner footsteps
As I approach the unmarked terrain of suffering.
Your compassionate presences assures me
That you will guide my intentions to be caring.
This day I join my heart with all living beings
As we walk together toward what lies ahead of us.

Joyce Rupp is well known for her work as a writer, spiritual midwife, international retreat leader, and conference speaker. She is the author of numerous bestselling books, including *Praying Our Goodbyes*, *Open the Door*, and *Fragments of Your Ancient Name*. *Fly While You Still Have Wings* earned an award in the spirituality books category from the Catholic Press Association. Rupp is a member of the Servite (Servants of Mary) community and the codirector of the Servite Center of Compassion's Boundless Compassion program. She lives in West Des Moines, Iowa.

www.authorjoycerupp.com
Facebook: joycerupp

Servite Center of Compassion: www.osms.org/servite-center-of-compassion

ALSO AVAILABLE

The definitive Christian guide to compassion, *Boundless Compassion* is the culmination of bestselling and award-winning author Joyce Rupp's research and work as codirector of the Servite Center of Compassionate Presence. Through this six-week personal transformation process for developing and deepening compassion, Rupp nudges, encourages, and inspires you to grow in the kind of love that motivated Jesus' life and mission for his disciples.

Available from Ave Maria Press or wherever books and e-books are sold.

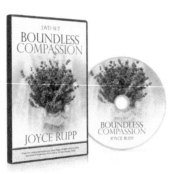

DVD Set

Also available is a set of five DVDs, each one containing an hour-long presentation by Joyce Rupp about one of the topics covered in *Boundless Compassion*. These teachings are a valuable resource for personal use, for small-group study, or for leading retreats and conferences on the subject of compassion.

These DVDs can be purchased from the www.osms.org gift shop or from www.joycerupp.com.